Made in the USA
Columbia, SC
04 May 2023

16096727R00063